THE STANLEY CUP FINAL

BY WENDY HINOTE LANIER

Apex is distributed by North Star Editions:
sales@northstareditions.com | 888-417-0195

Produced for Apex by Red Line Editorial.

Photographs ©: Phelan Ebenhack/AP Images, cover, 4–5, 6, 9, 29; Charles Krupa/AP Images, 1, 26–27; Shutterstock Images, 10–11, 15, 16–17; History and Art Collection/Alamy, 12–13; Chris O'Meara/AP Images, 18–19; Jason Franson/The Canadian Press/AP Images, 20; Ray Lussier/The Boston Herald/AP Images, 22–23; Elise Amendola/AP Images, 24–25

Library of Congress Control Number: 2022912149

ISBN
978-1-63738-294-3 (hardcover)
978-1-63738-330-8 (paperback)
978-1-63738-400-8 (ebook pdf)
978-1-63738-366-7 (hosted ebook)

Printed in the United States of America
Mankato, MN
012023

NOTE TO PARENTS AND EDUCATORS

Apex books are designed to build literacy skills in striving readers. Exciting, high-interest content attracts and holds readers' attention. The text is carefully leveled to allow students to achieve success quickly. Additional features, such as bolded glossary words for difficult terms, help build comprehension.

TABLE OF CONTENTS

CHAPTER 1

THE 2022 STANLEY CUP

It is Game 6 of the 2022 Stanley Cup Final. The Tampa Bay Lightning are facing the Colorado Avalanche. The score is 1–1.

Steven Stamkos scored for the Tampa Bay Lightning during Game 6 of the 2022 Stanley Cup Final.

An Avalanche player skates down the ice. He passes the puck to his teammate. His teammate passes again. The third player shoots. He scores!

FAST FACT

Nathan MacKinnon scored the Avalanche's first goal in Game 6. He helped with the second goal, too.

Artturi Lehkonen scored Colorado's second goal in Game 6.

The Avalanche hold on to the lead. They become National Hockey League (NHL) **champions**. Players celebrate on the ice.

HOISTING THE CUP

The Stanley Cup is 35 inches (89 cm) tall. It weighs close to 35 pounds (16 kg). Each player on the winning team gets to raise the Cup on the ice.

Avalanche superstar Cale Makar hoists the Stanley Cup in victory.

CHAPTER 2

STANLEY CUP HISTORY

The Stanley Cup contest began in Canada. Lord Frederick Stanley wanted to honor the best team. The Montreal Hockey Club won the first contest in 1893.

The Stanley Cup is the oldest prize in North American sports.

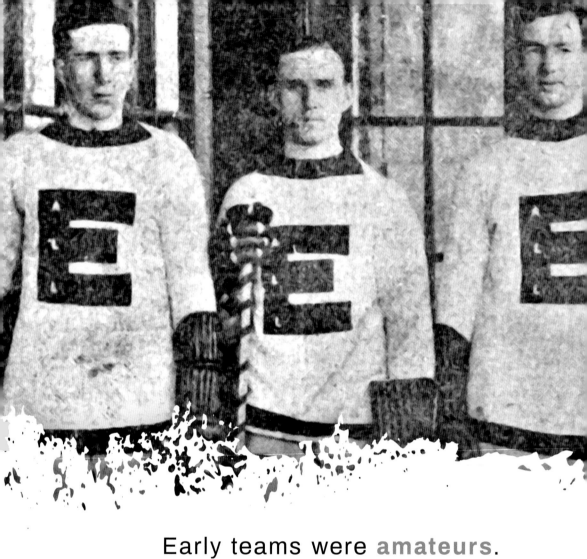

Early teams were amateurs.
That changed in 1910. The
National Hockey Association
(NHA) created a yearly
championship. Only pro teams
played.

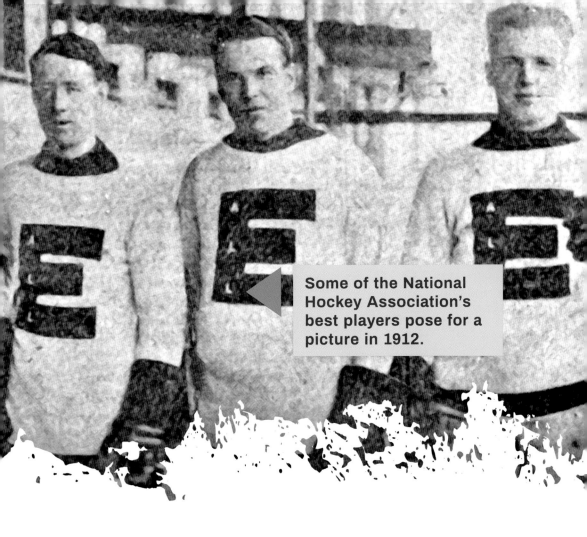

Some of the National Hockey Association's best players pose for a picture in 1912.

FAST FACT

The NHA was founded in 1909.

In 1917, the NHA became the NHL. The NHL includes Canadian and US teams. Starting in 1926, only NHL teams could play for the Stanley Cup.

UPDATING THE CUP

The original Stanley Cup was a silver bowl. But the Cup's design later changed. People added bands to the trophy. The names of winning players were engraved on them.

Champions take the Stanley Cup to the team's city. They show off the Cup during a parade.

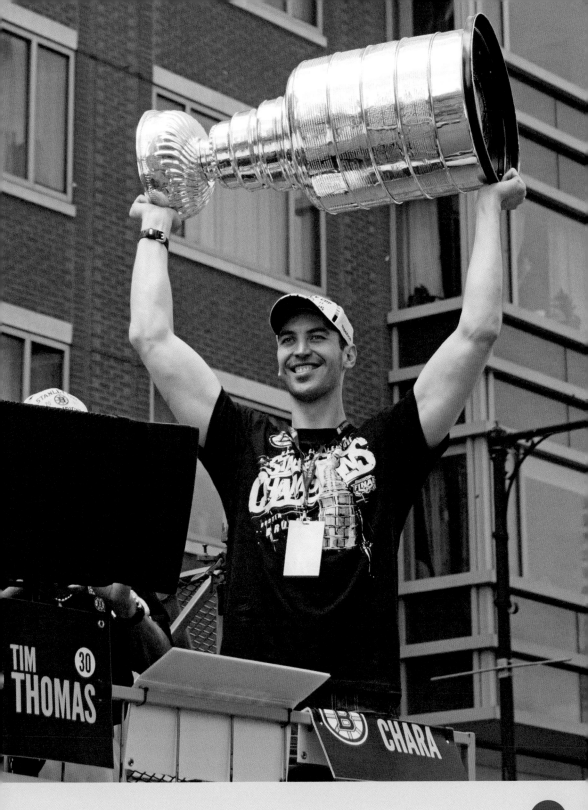

CHAPTER 3

MAKING THE FINAL

The NHL is split into two **conferences**. Each conference has two **divisions**. The best teams of each division make the **playoffs**. Some **wild-card teams** do, too.

The New York Islanders are part of the Metropolitan Division. That division is in the Eastern Conference.

The Florida Panthers lost in the second round of the 2022 playoffs.

The playoffs have four rounds. The first team to win four games wins the round. The losing team gets knocked out.

FAST FACT

A playoff round can be up to seven games long. It is known as a best-of-seven series.

Teams must win two rounds to reach their conference finals. Those finals are round three. Round four is the Stanley Cup Final.

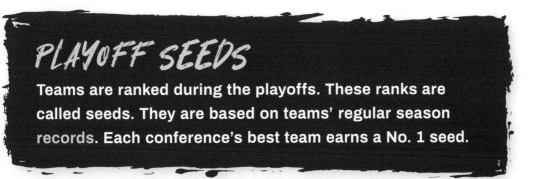

PLAYOFF SEEDS

Teams are ranked during the playoffs. These ranks are called seeds. They are based on teams' regular season records. Each conference's best team earns a No. 1 seed.

In the Stanley Cup Final, the Eastern Conference winner plays the Western Conference winner.

CHAPTER 4

BEST OF THE FINAL

Game 4 of the 1970 Stanley Cup Final went to **overtime**. Bobby Orr took a shot. He tripped, but the puck went in. His team became champions.

Bobby Orr's amazing shot helped the Boston Bruins win the 1970 Stanley Cup Final.

Bryan Bickell (29) celebrates scoring a goal in Game 6 of the 2013 Final.

During the 2013 Final, the Chicago Blackhawks trailed in Game 6. Then they scored two goals in 17 seconds. They won the Stanley Cup.

THE COMEBACK

The Toronto Maple Leafs started out badly in the 1942 Final. They lost the first three games. But they won the next four straight.

IOR

The St. Louis Blues formed in 1967. For more than 50 years, they never won a Stanley Cup. That finally changed in 2019.

FAST FACT

As of 2022, the Montreal Canadiens had won 24 Stanley Cups. That's far more than any other team.

St. Louis Blues players celebrate after winning the 2019 Stanley Cup Final.

COMPREHENSION QUESTIONS

Write your answers on a separate piece of paper.

1. Write a sentence that explains the main idea of Chapter 3.

2. Who is your favorite NHL player? Why?

3. Which team has won the most Stanley Cup Finals?

    A. Chicago Blackhawks

    B. Montreal Canadiens

    C. Tampa Bay Lightning

4. Which team won the 2019 Stanley Cup Final?

    A. Boston Bruins

    B. Colorado Avalanche

    C. St. Louis Blues

5. What does series mean in this book?

A playoff round can be up to seven games long. It is known as a best-of-seven series.

    A. a set of several games

    B. a team that loses

    C. a winning goal

6. What does straight mean in this book?

They lost the first three games. But they won the next four straight.

    A. not in real life

    B. over a long time

    C. in a row

Answer key on page 32.

GLOSSARY

amateurs
Athletes who do not get paid to play their sport.

champions
Teams that win the final game in a conference or league.

conferences
Smaller groups of teams within a sports league.

divisions
Groups of teams within a conference.

engraved
Cut or marked with words, often into metal or wood.

overtime
Time added to a game that is tied.

playoffs
A set of games played after the regular season to decide which team will be the champion.

records
The wins and losses that teams have during a season.

wild-card teams
Teams that are not at the top of their division but still did well.

TO LEARN MORE

BOOKS

Herman, Gail. *What Is the Stanley Cup?* New York: Penguin Workshop, 2019.

Morey, Allan. *The Stanley Cup Finals*. Minneapolis: Bellwether Media, 2019.

Scheff, Matt. *The Stanley Cup Finals: Hockey's Greatest Tournament.* Minneapolis: Lerner Publications, 2021.

ONLINE RESOURCES

Visit **www.apexeditions.com** to find links and resources related to this title.

ABOUT THE AUTHOR

Wendy Hinote Lanier is a Texan and a former elementary teacher who writes and speaks for children and adults. She is the author of more than 45 books for children on topics related to science, technology, social studies, the arts, and, of course, Texas.

INDEX

ANSWER KEY:
1. Answers will vary; 2. Answers will vary; 3. B; 4. C; 5. A; 6. C